W9-CHU-176

DRUGS AND YOUR PARENTS

It is lonely being the child of a chemically dependent parent.

THE DRUG ABUSE PREVENTION LIBRARY

DRUGS AND YOUR PARENTS

Rhoda McFarland

CHAVEZ HIGH SCHOOL
LIBRARY
HOUSTON, TEXAS

THE ROSEN PUBLISHING GROUP, INC.
NEW YORK

The people pictured in this book are only models. They in no way practice or endorse the activities illustrated. Captions serve only to explain the subjects of photographs and do not in any way imply a connection between the real-life models and the staged situations.

Published in 1991, 1993, 1997 by the Rosen Publishing Group, Inc.
29 East 21st Street, New York, NY 10010

Revised Edition 1997

Copyright © 1991, 1993, 1997 by the Rosen Publishing Group, Inc.

All rights reserved. No part of this book may be reproduced in any form without permission in writing from the publisher, except by a reviewer.

Library of Congress Cataloging-in-Publication Data

McFarland, Rhoda
  Drugs and your parents / Rhoda McFarland
  (The Drug Abuse Prevention Library)
  Includes bibliographical references and index.
  Summary: Readers who have a parent or parents that are
    alcohol/drug abusers learn how to survive in a chemically
    dependent household, and find out where to get help for their
    parent(s) and themselves.
  ISBN 0-8239-2603-6
  1. Children of alcoholics—Juvenile literature. 2. Children of narcotic
    addicts—Juvenile literature. 3. Parent and teenager—juvenile
    literature. [1. Alcoholism. 2. Drug abuse. 3. Parent and child.]
    I. Title. II. Series.
  HV5066.M35 1991
  362.29'13—dc20   91-9188
                                          CIP
                                          AC

Manufactured in the United States of America

Contents

Introduction

*M*ike worried that his father would hurt his mother in a drunken rage. Danielle was embarrassed because everyone knew her mother got high and slept around. Tina refused to go back to school because the teachers knew her father and brother were arrested for selling cocaine.

As a young person with a chemically dependent parent, you grow up fast. You are forced to take on more responsibilities than you should. And you are forced to make adult decisions alone.

The purpose of this book is to help young people with drug-abusing parents make positive decisions. We will discuss how chemical dependence—which includes drug addiction and alcoholism—affects the family. We will also talk about

Facts

- About 43 percent of adults in the U.S. have been exposed to alcoholism in the family.
- Almost one in five adult Americans lived with an alcoholic while growing up.
- Children of alcoholics are at a higher risk to marry into alcoholic families.
- Children of alcoholics are three times more likely to be admitted to a hospital for substance-abuse treatment.
- Children of alcoholics often have difficulties in school.
- Eighty percent of family violence is drug related.
- Forty to 60 percent of all child abuse is related to alcohol and other drugs.
- There are about 27 million children of alcoholics in the US. Between 7 and 11 million are thought to be under eighteen.
- Thirteen to 25 percent of all children of alcoholics are likely to become alcoholics.

family violence and ways to protect yourself from harm. Most importantly, this book will provide you with information on how to take care of yourself and get help.

There are people in your school and community who understand drug abuse. They are ready to share their experience, strength, and hope with you. The help list on page 58 is a place to start looking for the support and aid that can end your confusion and loneliness.

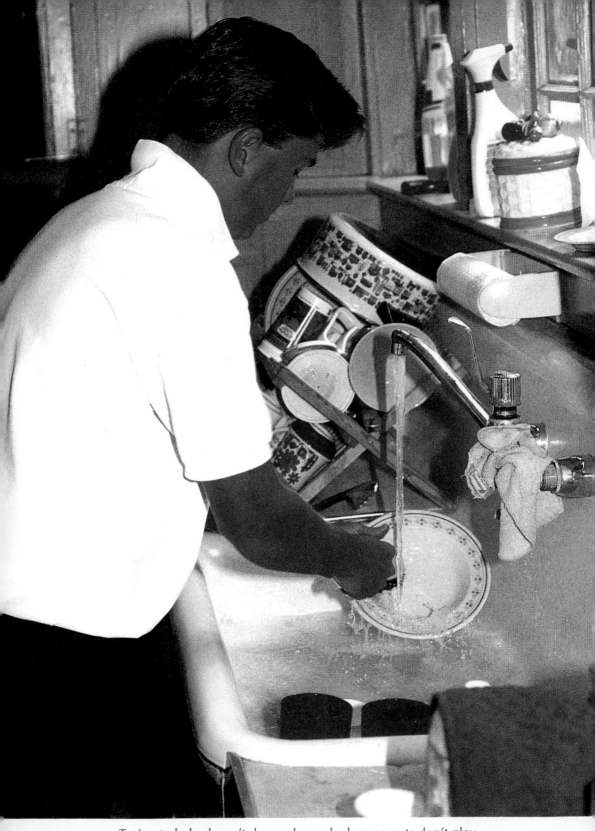

Trying to help doesn't do much good when parents don't play their part.

CHAPTER 1

Chemical Dependence

Stacy's mother and Michael, her boy-friend, liked to stay out at a local bar for hours. Although Stacy hated being home alone, she sometimes thought it was better when they weren't there. At home, if they weren't yelling at each other, they were yelling at her. After school Stacy cleaned the house, picked up her younger brother from school, and cooked dinner. After all that, Michael would call Stacy a lazy slob.

When Eric was young, he and his father drove into the city together every week. He didn't know what his father was doing those nights in the city. His father would drive to the same garage, park the car, and tell Eric to wait in the car. Now that he was older, Eric knew his father

10 was buying drugs. Eric liked it better when he didn't understand.

More than 11 million young people under eighteen have parents who abuse drugs. Many drug-abusing parents are in denial and refuse to see that they have a problem. It can be scary to have a parent dependent on a drug. Someone who is chemically dependent on drugs is called an addict. Someone who is addicted to alcohol is called an alcoholic.

Addiction to alcohol or other drugs is chemical dependence. And chemical dependence is a disease. Like other diseases it has symptoms. Two of the more common symptoms include denial and sudden mood swings.

- Stacy's mom denies that she has a problem when Stacy says she is concerned about her drinking. Stacy's mom says that she doesn't *need* to drink, she just likes to after a stressful day at work. Stacy's mother is in denial.
- Eric's father often returned to the car nervous and distracted. Other times he was relaxed. He would smile, and stop for a soda. Eric was confused and scared.

Eric's father and Stacy's mother have lost control of their chemical use. The chemical controls them. Through the continued use of drugs and alcohol, they have developed both a physical and psychological need for the drug. Both their bodies and their minds now depend on the drug in order to function.

Chemical dependence is a primary disease. This means that problems don't cause chemical dependence; chemical dependence causes problems. One drink after work will not make the job any easier. One hit of marijuana to start the day will not make the bills go away. Using drugs to solve your problems only makes a situation worse or creates new problems. If you have any other problems, you cannot deal with them until the chemical use is stopped.

The disease of chemical dependence worsens over time. As the user's tolerance increases, so does his or her consumption of the drug. Sometimes this leads the user to try more dangerous drugs in order to achieve a better high. Without help, the cycle continues. With help, chemical dependence can be stopped.

12 | ## Who Is at Risk?

No one knows what causes chemical dependence. Not everyone who drinks alcohol or uses drugs becomes addicted. But we do know that alcoholism runs in families. Research shows that children of alcoholics are more likely to become chemically dependent. Sons of alcoholics are four times more likely than other men to become alcoholics. Daughters of alcoholics are three times more likely than other women to become alcoholics. Women from alcoholic families are more likely to marry alcoholic men, thus continuing the cycle of the disease.

Studies show that teens are at higher risk for drug use if they have a drug-abusing sibling. It may be that the drug user is looking for a drug-using buddy at home. It may also be that an accessible source of drugs makes it easier for another family member to begin using. It is important to know that chemical dependence in the family raises your risk for becoming dependent.

Does Your Parent Have a Drug Problem?

Your parents do not have to be drunk or high at every moment to be addicted. Addiction has to do with getting the

If you get rid of their supply, they know how to get more.

drug, using the drug, and trying to live a normal life. It is not how much or how often people use drugs. The important thing is what happens to them when they do. Here are questions to ask yourself:

- Do you worry about your parents' chemical use?
- Have you ever been embarrassed by it?
- Are most of your parents' friends users or heavy drinkers?
- Do you ever lie to cover up your parents' drug use?
- Have your parents ever forgotten what happened while they were drunk or high?
- Do your parents avoid parties where they can't get alcohol or other drugs?

13

14

- Do you ever feel guilty about your parents' drug use?
- Do your parents make excuses about their drug use?
- Do your parents sometimes say they are sorry after drinking or using drugs?
- Do your parents ever hide drugs or alcohol around the house?
- Have you ever been afraid of what your parents might do while drunk or high?
- Have you ever been afraid to ride in a car with your parents when they had been drinking or using?

If you answered yes to any of these questions, it may be a sign that your parent has a problem. It is best to seek further help through a counselor or Al-Anon before approaching your parents. A counselor can help you better understand your feelings and talk about ways to cope with your situation.

What Can You Do?

What can you do? Remember the three C's. You didn't *cause* their disease. You can't *control* it. You can't *cure* it. You *can* stop blaming yourself. You *can* stop covering up for your parents. You *can* find help for yourself.

What's Going On in This House?

Mark was proud to take his report card home. After failing three classes last semester, he had worked hard to earn all B's and C's. But instead of the praise he expected, Mark's father yelled at him for the two C's. Then his dad stormed out of the room carrying a half-empty bottle.

Susan knew that her class needed her answer about the senior trip. She wanted to go, but her mother was unpredictable. One day she might say yes, the next she would say no.

When her little brother said, "Daddy's acting funny again," Jennifer wanted to go to a friend's house. But she was afraid to leave her little brother alone with him.

Mark's father is an alcoholic. Susan's mother is hooked on prescription drugs. Jennifer's father is a cocaine addict.

16 All three teenagers live with the uncertainty of chemical dependence. They never know what to expect. They can't depend on anything. Moods change in a minute. What was a happy, pleasant time is suddenly tense and unhappy.

Kathy's father promised not to drink before the game. She couldn't understand why he broke his promise.

John's father promised to go fishing with him last weekend. Instead he went to the ball game with some guys from work.

The last time Larry's mother got high on speed and was gone for three days, she promised not to do it again. She has been gone two days so far this time. Mandy's father promised to be home early. He didn't just forget her birthday dinner. He forgot to come home at all.

Broken promises break hearts. No matter how often it happens, you always hope that *this* time will be different. Maybe it has happened so many times that you don't expect anything anymore. It doesn't seem to hurt as much when you don't count on it.

Living that way creates confusion. You don't know what to do. You can't figure out what behavior is right. When promises are broken all the time you think you

You never know what to expect when a parent is out of control on drugs.

18 must be doing something wrong. There's no one to help you sort things out. Your family has the "Don't Talk" rule. You never talk to each other or anyone else about what is going on at home. You may have been told not to talk. You may be afraid that your friends won't understand. Maybe you're embarrassed and think your friends won't like you if they know what goes on in your house. You keep it all inside, and the confusion gets worse.

When Mandy's father finally came home, her mother screamed at him. They had a terrible fight. Mandy felt that it was her fault because it was her birthday dinner they were fighting about. Jeff is sixteen. He hates it when his parents fight. He's afraid that his father will kill his mother. That fear has been part of Jeff since he was a little kid with the covers over his head in the middle of the night.

A constant war goes on in chemically dependent homes. Even when your parents are not fighting, you can feel the tension. You know that a fight can break out at any time. That kind of tension makes everyone ready for a fight. Seeing parents argue and fight teaches the family how to mistreat each other. It's no wonder you fight with your brothers and sisters.

Maybe you get into arguments at school   **19**
and with your friends. That's not unusual
for young people who live in chemically
dependent homes.

Broken promises, fighting, not being
able to depend on anyone at home make
you afraid to trust others. You don't want
more disappointment. Not being able to
trust others makes you feel that you must
do everything yourself. You learn to depend on yourself. Making everything turn
out right is very important. But in your
house you can't make everything right. No
matter how hard you try, you can't please
your parent. Again, you keep it all inside.
You keep the second rule of a chemically
dependent family—"Don't trust."

Because you keep everything inside,
you think you're the only one with a family
like yours. What is going on in your house
is going on in the homes of four to six
teenagers in every classroom in your
school. They're just as confused as you
are. They don't know what is going on at
home. Most of all, they don't know what is
going on inside themselves. Like you, they
have learned the third rule in a chemically
dependent home—"Don't Feel."

Homework is even harder when parental battles are going on.

CHAPTER 3

What's Going On Inside ME?

O h, how she hated it when they screamed at each other. Mandy lay on the bed with her head buried in the pillow. She knew the neighbors could hear her parents fighting. It was so embarrassing. What must they think? She was so afraid that one of her friends might come by the house and hear them. She would just die if they did. She never asked anyone over because she didn't know how her father would act. When he was in a bad mood it was awful. She never knew when he might come home drunk. She didn't want people to know. They just wouldn't understand.

CHAVEZ HIGH SCHOOL
LIBRARY
HOUSTON, TEXAS

22   She has been gone two days this time. Larry doesn't know when his mother will be home. He is always afraid that when she leaves she won't come back. It is hard to concentrate on his homework. He can't think about anything else. Maybe she will be found dead some-where. Maybe she will take off with someone and forget all about him. Maybe she will . . . Larry's mind goes crazy when his mother is gone.

The anger in his father worries Jeff. He is afraid that his father will lose control and do something terrible. When his father isn't high on cocaine, he acts even worse. He gets really mean. There is a knot of worry in his stomach all the time.

Fear

Young people in chemically dependent homes live in constant fear and stress. Mandy was sure people could tell what was going on in her home. She never talked about what went on. She kept the "Don't Talk" rule. So she didn't know that Kathy, Jeff, Larry, Mike, and many others have felt the same way. She didn't know she wasn't the only one.

All young people are afraid they won't be liked. Having your friends like you is very important. Most teenagers handle their fears by sharing with others. They talk to friends about their problems. They share school activities and parties. They visit each other's homes. When they are troubled they know they can get support from their family. Young people like Mandy and Larry don't have that support at home. They think something is wrong with them. They never think that something is wrong with the home. Nothing is wrong with Mandy. She deserves the support and safety that parents give. Her parents are too messed up by chemicals to give it. Because of that, Mandy thinks, "If my friends really knew me they wouldn't like me."

Fear is part of life for teenagers whose parents abuse drugs. It never goes away. Larry worries about his mother even when she's at home. The next time she can get drugs will be all it takes. He knows she will be gone again. He is afraid something will happen and she'll never come back. He hates her sometimes for using drugs and treating him badly. But he doesn't want to be left alone.

24 Jeff and Mandy hate the fighting. They don't know why their parents stay together when they fight that way. But the thought of one leaving is terrible too.

Besides being afraid that his parents will separate, Jeff is afraid that his father will kill his mother. Once Jeff stopped his father from hitting her with a fireplace poker. Jeff is afraid of what might happen when he isn't home. He worries that his little brother will get in his father's way. Living with his father's anger makes Jeff feel alone and different from other teens.

Loneliness

Keeping the "Don't Talk" rule makes Jeff, Mandy, and Larry feel alone. No one in the family talks about what's going on. They are alone in their home. They don't talk to people outside for fear of not being liked. Hiding their feelings, they feel all alone with their troubles. They think they are different from anyone else. They look the same, but they feel different inside.

Anger

Young people whose parents are chemically dependent live with their parents' anger. They also feel angry themselves.

The "Don't Talk" rule makes for a lonely life.

Jeff and Mandy hear yelling and screaming. Jeff fears that his father will hurt someone physically. Many homes are filled with terror of a parent who beats the children or the other parent. Doors are knocked down. Holes are kicked in walls. The children learn that being angry means being violent.

Mandy learned when she was little not to show anger. Her parents could scream and yell, but no one else could. She learned to hold her anger inside.

25

26   Anger held inside can cause stomachaches, headaches, and other stress-related illnesses. It makes teens act out anger in other ways. Jeff gets into fights at school. He argues with teachers. He is always in trouble.

Holding in her anger keeps Mandy from doing her best in school. She just can't get moving. She feels bad about herself. She would like to talk about her feelings but she is afraid.

You need to let out your anger in ways that don't hurt you or anyone else. It's okay to be angry. Your parents aren't there for you when you need comfort. You hate their chemical abuse. You feel as though you live in a zoo. You hate feeling different because of them. Yes, you *are* angry. But there are healthy ways to relieve your anger.

- Talk to someone you trust, such as a relative, a teacher, or friend.
- Go for a run or try some other athletic activity.
- Write your frustrations in a journal or a special notebook.
- Meditate.
- Hit a pillow or punching bag.

Think about what you're really angry about. It is the disease that makes your parents the way they are. It's the disease that is messing up your life. Get mad at the disease. That will help you see your parents differently. It will help you feel better about being in your family. The disease is causing you pain.

Guilt

Along with being angry, you wish the dependent parent were gone. Many teens wish the parent dead. Some think of ways to get rid of the parent. Then they feel guilty for having those feelings. It is natural to want to be rid of what causes you pain. You're not a bad person for having those feelings. You're human. You're like every other teenager who is living in an addicted family.

Young people often feel guilty about what is happening at home. Larry thought it was his fault that his mother didn't come home. He tried to do everything she wanted. No matter what he did, it wasn't the right thing. He felt guilty because he couldn't find the right thing to do.

You may feel guilty because your parents say it's your fault they drink. Maybe

28 they call you names. Being unable to make them stop makes you feel guilty. Remember the three C's: You didn't cause it; you can't control it; you can't cure it.

You must break the "Don't Talk," "Don't Trust," and "Don't Feel" rules. You may have tried to hide your feelings, but found it difficult. Talk about your feelings to someone you trust.

Shame

When Mandy sees her father staggering down the street, she crosses to the other side. She is afraid that he will stop her and someone will see. She is ashamed and embarrassed by his behavior.

Jeff could not bring his friends home. He didn't know how his father would act. Sometimes his father would be friendly. Other times he would criticize Jeff in front of his friends. Once he had even made fun of a friend's haircut. Jeff was so embarrassed that he quit having friends over. He hated feeling ashamed.

When Larry's mother wasn't using speed, she was drinking. She was often too high to do anything. Larry had to do many chores, such as clean the house.

He learned to wash his clothes himself. *29*
The nurse in elementary school had
noticed how dirty he was. She told him
to bathe every day. She helped him learn
to take care of himself. His mother never
seemed to notice if he was clean or not.
He still felt embarrassed and ashamed
about how dirty he used to be.

Young people who live in a chemically
dependent home often feel ashamed
about their parents and their homes.
They may eventually grow to be ashamed
of themselves. Shame makes you hate
yourself. It makes your feel "dirty." You
feel unworthy of anyone's love. In doing
that, you have confused what your
parents do with who you are. You are
not your father or mother. What they do
is not you. You need support from people
who understand your feelings. You can
find such people in support groups.
Teens in support groups share your
problems. One such group is Alateen. It is
a support group for teens whose lives
have been affected by alcoholics. Call
one of the numbers listed in the help
section of this book for help in finding a
support group that suits your needs.

When one parent is addicted the other is forced to deal with many problems alone.

CHAPTER 4

The Codependent Parent

*R*ita stared at the open book. She hadn't turned a page in the last thirty minutes. She heard her mother's complaints through the walls of her bedroom. Why did her father put up with it? Rita was tired of doing all the housework while her mother stayed in bed. "Nerves," her father told Rita when she asked. At first she didn't mind helping out, but now it seemed like it was never going to end. Her mother was constantly demanding water to help her swallow her pills. Rita's father tried to make his wife happy, but she found something wrong with everything he did. Sometimes Rita wanted to scream at him, "Why do you let her do that to you?"

32 "You'll have to ask your father." Steve should have known his mother wouldn't make a decision alone. She checked everything with his father, from dinner menus, to Steve's weekend activities, to whether or not it was okay to visit her own mom in the evenings. She would not make a move without his father's permission. If his father thought she disobeyed in any way, he would punish her and the whole family would suffer. Steve wanted to leave as soon as possible. He had stopped feeling sorry for his mother and was now both angry and ashamed. Why didn't she ever stand up to him? Didn't she have a mind of her own?

Codependent Parents

People who have chemically dependent parents are forced to find ways—often unhealthy ways—to cope with what's happening in the family. In many cases, the other family members learn to put the needs of the abuser before their own needs. This may mean making excuses, or taking on extra responsibility, in order to maintain the appearance of a normal family.

While it is okay to help out sometimes,

when it becomes a pattern it is called codependency. Rita's father, Jim, is a codependent. He made excuses for his wife and counted upon his daughter to take on the extra responsibilities. He only felt good about himself when his wife was happy. He depended on the acceptance of his wife in the same way that she depended on her drug. This behavior is dangerous and unhealthy.

As the alcoholism of Steve's father worsens, so does the codependence of Steve's mother. She takes over more and more of the household responsibilities while still working a full-time job. She works hard to pay all of the household's bills and worries constantly about her husband. She attempts to cover for him, assuming responsibility for the entire family. She has let go of her own needs and desires in order to take care of those of her husband.

Worrying about the dependent person makes the codependent neglect the family. One of the children usually takes over the job of parenting. Often the children feel the parents' neglect and take out their anger on each other.

34   At first, codependents make excuses for the dependent's behavior. They call in and say the person is sick when he's really hung over. They deny there's a problem. The codependent begins to get more and more angry. Then the nagging and fighting begin. If there is no fighting, the anger is there just the same. It is like living with a time bomb. Some homes are quiet and dead. Everyone is empty of feeling.

Living that way makes people behave strangely. Your codependent parents try very hard to control the drinking and what happens in the family. The harder they try, the worse things get. They feel very guilty because they can't control what goes on. Finally, they realize that they can't control themselves. They need help as much as the dependent.

You live in the same confusion, and you need help too. Learning to take care of yourself is very important. Alateen can help you do that. Your school counselor may have a list of places where you can get help. The school nurse often knows about groups in the community. Begin to look around for help. Talking about it with someone you can trust is your first step.

CHAPTER 5

What's Your Role in the Family?

Getting through the day in a chemically dependent home is a struggle. It's as though each person is playing a part in a mixed-up play. Roles are played out in the family.

Super-Good-Responsible

Everyone thinks Randy is perfect. He gets straight As. He is president of his class, captain of the basketball team, and works at a hardware store on the weekends. He takes care of the house and his younger sisters. Randy should feel great about himself. But he doesn't. He thinks of what he could do better if only he tried harder. He feels like he'll never be good enough to be appreciated by his parents. Randy is angry about living in such a

36 screwed-up family. He tries to keep on top of everything, but it is nearly impossible. Randy plays the role of the Super-Good-Responsible kid.

Super-Bad-Irresponsible Troublemaker

Sandy gets plenty of attention from her parents. But it is all negative. She is as bad as Randy is good. Sandy doesn't mean to be bad, but she can't seem to help it. She never does her chores. She doesn't let anyone know where she is going. She is failing classes and has started cutting school to hang out with her friends. She just doesn't want to try anything. It looks as though she likes being bad, but she feels guilty inside. She is angry with her mother for drinking and never being around except to yell at her. But most of all, Sandy is angry with herself for being so messed-up. She wants to be a good kid, but there doesn't seem to be any real point in it. Sandy has assumed the role of the Super-Bad-Irresponsible Troublemaker.

Flexible Adjuster

Shana doesn't count on anything. She just goes with the flow. She knows her parents are unreliable, so she has learned to rely on herself. She can adjust to any

The Super-Good-Responsible kid tries to do it all.

You have to be a Flexible Adjuster when your mother lies down on the job.

situation. She can take care of herself. Nothing bothers Shana, or so it seems. In reality, Shana is angry at her parents for not being there for her. Not being able to count on anything makes her furious. Her mother might be in the house, but she sure isn't around for Shana. And her father never wants to talk about it. To deal with her family, Shana became a Flexible Adjuster.

Comedian

The tension in Jason's house was driving him crazy. For as long as he could remember, his parents fought behind closed doors, but didn't say a word to each other in front of anyone else. Jason was confused and scared. He didn't know what was going on. As a little boy, he would break tension by doing something funny. Everyone, including Jason, would feel better. Even today Jason covers his real feelings by laughter and jokes. He is angry at what happens in his house. Jason continues making others laugh because it's the only way he knows how to keep things normal. He is the Comedian.

Invisible Loner

David has no friends. He never learned how to make them. He doesn't spend very much time with his family. He feels lonely and very different from everyone else. When he was young, David's parents were too caught up in themselves to take much notice of David. He learned to take care of himself. He played by himself, read to himself, watched TV by himself. He never got in the way, so no one paid any attention to him. He feels worthless and unimportant. David's role is the Invisible Loner.

Many teenagers in chemically dependent homes fit these roles. Some see themselves in two of the roles. You don't have to stay locked in a role. You can get help to deal with your feelings. Break the "Don't Talk" rule. Let others help you.

When your home is full of violence, the anger may rub off on you.

CHAPTER 6

Family Violence

David's hands shook as he reached for the phone. The voice in his head said, "He'll be mad if he finds out." That fear had stopped David before, but this time David was afraid for his younger brother. Someone was going to get hurt if he didn't do something. He dialed a teen hot line number. "I'm afraid my mom's boyfriend is going to hurt someone. He uses drugs and drinks a lot . . . ." The person on the hot line listened to David's story and gave him the number for the Domestic Violence Center. The counselor there helped David make a safety plan.

Creating Your Own Safety Plan

If you live with violence in your home, here are some ideas for a safety plan.

- Talk to someone you trust.

41

42

- Find a safe place to go. Ask a friend or relative to take you in when you fear your parent is becoming violent.
- Create a code word that you can give to a trusted adult. If you need to call that person for help, the code word will signal that you are in trouble, but not alert or anger the abusive parent.
- Never argue with or contradict the angry parent. Leave the house when the abusive parent is angry.
- Learn the numbers of a domestic abuse agency, doctor, or trusted adult. Record them in your own address book.
- If you fear that you or someone else is in danger, *call the police*. Don't worry about what anyone else will think. Be safe.

David was afraid someone would be hurt physically, but there are many other forms of abuse. Being left home alone, locked in a closet, or deprived of food are considered neglect. Being insulted, degraded, and sworn at are forms of emotional abuse. The hurt from neglect and emotional abuse lasts long after bruises are gone.

There are agencies in your town or city to help you. Look in the yellow pages under Crisis Intervention, Domestic Abuse, or Family Services. Your school counselor can also tell you where to get help.

In most states, when you tell certain adults—a teacher, school official, doctor, nurse, therapist, police officer, or domestic violence advocate—that you are being abused, they are considered mandated reporters. That means they are required by law to report the abuse to the child protective services in your area. If you are not yet comfortable with having your abuse reported, then you can call a domestic violence agency and ask for help anonymously. However, don't let the fear of a parent or other adult getting in trouble keep you in an unsafe situation. You deserve to live without fear of harm.

Sexual Abuse

One of the biggest secrets in some chemically dependent families is sexual abuse. Many people think of forced sexual intercourse as the only form of sexual abuse, but there are many other examples as well. You may be the victim of sexual abuse without even realizing it.

Sharon hated it when her father made her sit in his lap. He'd put his hands all over her and feel her breasts.

44

Carl tried to be out when his Aunt Hazel visited. She gave him wet kisses on the mouth. It made him feel dirty.

Sue's uncle would stand at the end of the hall and unzip his pants and tell her that he had something special to show her.

Jim's mother sometimes left her door open and stood naked so he could see her.

Carol's stepbrother walked close to her, and whispered in her ear, "You have a nice butt."

All of these young people were sexually abused. No one has the right to touch your body if you don't want to be touched. No one has the right to expose sexual parts to you, or to say things that make you feel uncomfortable. It's important for you to know that you are not to blame for what has happened to you. The adult is responsible for betraying your trust.

You may need help handling the situation. Call your local teen hot line. Talk to your school counselor. Look in the yellow pages under Crisis Intervention and Mental Health Services. You need to talk to someone who understands and learn that there is help.

Dealing with Your Dependent Parent

*N*ikki rushed into the room, frustrated and out of breath. She sat down in the group circle and began to explain, "I was already running late when I went out to my car this morning. I couldn't believe it when I saw that my father had parked right behind me after coming home drunk last night. I was so angry! How could he be so selfish? As I started to shake him awake, I thought about some of the things we had talked about in group and decided against it. At least he isn't hurting anyone when he sleeps. So I took the bus this morning, that's why I'm late." The group laughed but understood Nikki's frustration and fear. Everyone there had a parent who abused alcohol or other drugs. They met every week at

46 school. With their counselor, they talked about the problems of living with chemically dependent parents. By talking about her father, Nikki didn't feel so helpless and alone.

Taking Control

At times Nikki felt like a helpless victim. You may be a victim, but you are not helpless. Take control of yourself, and responsibility for your life. Do things to help you lead a more independent and healthy life. It's not easy, but you can do it. It helps to have a support system like Nikki's. Find a group or someone you trust to help you through the hard times.

Things Not to Do

• *Don't blame*. Don't blame your parents for drinking or doing drugs. Don't blame them for everything that goes wrong. Don't blame yourself for everything that goes wrong in the house. Blaming keeps every-one helpless. Nothing good happens when you blame.

• *Don't take things personally*. When your parents yell at you, it's the disease talking. Your parents hurt too. Get mad at the disease, not at them.

Meeting with peers in a support group can help when things are hard at home.

48

• *Don't cover for your parents.* Don't make excuses. Don't lie for them. Don't call the boss and say they're sick. Don't drag your father into the house when he passes out on the lawn. Don't put your mother to bed when she's too drunk to do it herself. Covering makes it easier for them to keep using drugs.

• *Don't try to control the drug use.* Getting rid of the supply won't help. They'll just get more. Don't ask them to promise not to drink or use. Don't look for them and try to bring them home. Their drug use can't be controlled until they get help.

• *Don't withdraw from others.* As the chemical dependence gets worse in your home, you may not want to be around others. You feel no one will like you because of your parents. You need to be with people. You need your friends to help you get your mind off your troubles. You need to talk to someone you trust. Don't let the disease make you a prisoner.

• *Don't try to talk to your parents when they've been drinking or using.* They're out of their minds then. You'd be talking to a chemical, not a person.

• *Don't feel ashamed and try to cover it up.* Don't tell lies about how wonderful everything is in your family. Don't laugh and pretend it's funny. *You are not your parents. Your parents are not you.* Nothing is wrong with you. Be proud of YOU.

• *Don't ride with a parent who has been drinking alcohol or using drugs.* Your parent may be angry if you won't get in the car.

• *Don't drink or use drugs yourself.* You see your parents trying to escape their prob-lems by drinking or using. You may want to use drugs to escape your problems too. DON'T. Your chances of becoming chemically dependent are too high.

Things to Do

• *Treat your parents with dignity and respect.* You may think they don't deserve it. If you yell at your parents, you won't feel good about *you.* You deserve to treat yourself better.

• *Go to support groups.* When you join a support group, you have the opportunity to meet others who share your problem. They understand what you are going through with your parent because they have the same problems.

• *Have outside interests.* Get your mind off what is wrong and onto what is right. You deserve to be happy. The only one

50 | who can make you happy is you. Take responsibility for doing things that are good for you. Get involved in activities that are healthy and fun.

• *Let your parents know you love them.* Chemically dependent parents hate themselves. They don't think they're lovable at all. They need to know you care. Tell them when you know they haven't been drinking or using.

• *Be sure you and your family are safe.* Have a plan for your safety. If a parent gets violent go to a safe place. If you feel uncomfortable going to a neighbor or a friend in the middle of the night, GO ANYWAY. Being safe is the most important thing. Have two copies of a list of emergency phone numbers. Keep one with you, and leave one in a safe place at home. Include these numbers: a relative or friend who will come to help you, the fire department, the police, the children's center where you can stay, your doctor, and an ambulance service. If you are on the 911 system, that one number will put you in touch with all emergency services.

• *Learn all you can about chemical dependence.* The more you know about the disease, the more you'll understand yourself and your family.

• *Be good to yourself.* Your family
doesn't give you the support and love you
deserve. It's important that you learn to be
loving to yourself. You can learn to tell
yourself the positive things you need to
hear. You can be your own best friend.
Get up each morning, look at yourself in
the mirror, and say:

I am lovable.
I respect myself.
I am special.
I am a caring person.
I am worthwhile.
I'm okay today.
I deserve only good things.
I am happy with myself.
I deserve to be happy.
I am my best friend.
It's okay if I'm not perfect.
I am capable and confident.
I like myself.
It's okay to please myself.
I am important.
I feel good about myself.
I am a good person.
I am the best me I can be.

Your world has been a world of pain and
confusion. You may not live in a happy
family, but you can be a happy person.

Having someone you trust to talk with can ease even a bad
situation.

CHAPTER 8

Help Yourself

*H*eather knew she could get her paper done if she got up early. It was hard to find time to do everything. Her brother and sister depended on her to do the cooking, cleaning, and shopping. Even with all the responsibilities at home, Heather still managed to make honor roll. She only wished someone would be proud of her achievements.

Heather felt frustrated when her friends went out on weekends without her. But she had too many responsibilities and there wasn't any time left for friends. Her father worked during the day. When he was home, he drank. Heather was sick of taking care of everyone else. She wished someone would take care of her.

56 are younger children, how will they be affected?

The safest way to get your questions answered is by calling a drug abuse or teen crisis line in your town. You don't have to give your name. Find out if your situation is one that must be reported by law. If you are not comfortable reporting it, ask the hot line who you can call for support. If it does not need to be reported, ask if there is a counselor with whom you can talk.

If you or a family member is in danger, the most important thing is your safety. Take action now. Call the police. If you aren't in danger, take the time to get help in making your decision.

To Use or Not to Use Chemicals

The greatest abusers of chemicals are children of abusers. You may say that you won't be like your parents. However, according to the National Association for Children of Alcoholics (NACOA), 13 to 25 percent of all children of alcoholics are likely to become alcoholics.

Thad drinks at parties. He says he can control it. His attitude may let him deny the signs of a problem in the future.

Everyone knows Jenny's parents are alcoholics. Her friends were surprised when they saw her drinking at a party. Jenny didn't want her new boyfriend to think she wasn't cool. She felt guilty, but she chose to do it anyway.

Bill steers clear of drugs. His uncles are alcoholics. His grandfather died from alcoholism. His brother is strung out on crack. He is sure that he will become chemically dependent if he ever gets close to alcohol or other drugs.

You know that you are at high risk for chemical dependence if your parents are chemically dependent. Your fears and attitudes about alcohol and other drugs make you more susceptible to addiction. How can you tell if you will be dependent yourself? You can't. How can you be sure that you won't be chemically dependent? Don't drink or use drugs.

Help Yourself

Growing up in a drug-dependent home can be lonely and confusing, but it doesn't have to stay that way. Help yourself to a better life by reaching out to others for help. Use the Help List on the next page to start on your way to a happier tomorrow.

Where to Go for Help

Al-Anon/Alateen Family
   Groups
1600 Corporate Landing
   Parkway
Virginia Beach, VA 23454
(800) 356-9996 (hot line)
Web site: http://www.al-
   anon.alateen.org

Childhelp USA
(800) 422-4453 (hot line)

Children of Alcoholics
   Foundation
555 Madison Avenue
New York, NY 10022
(800) 359-COAF

National Association for
   Children of Alcoholics
11426 Rockville Pike
Rockville, MD 20652
(888) 554-2627 (hot line)
Web site: http://www.
   health.org/NACOA

National Clearing House for
   Alcohol and Drug
   Information
P.O. Box 2345

Rockville, MD 21852
(800) 729-6686 (hot line)
Web site: http://www.
   health.org

National Council on
   Alcoholism and Drug
   Dependence
12 West 21st Street
New York, NY 10010
(800) 622-2255 (hot line)
(212) 206-6770
Web site: http://www.
   ncadd.org

IN CANADA

Alcohol and Drug
   Dependency Information
   and Counseling Services
#2, 2471 1/2 Portage Avenue
Winnipeg, M R3J 0N6
(204) 942-4730

Richmond Alcohol and Drug
   Abuse Team
170-5720 Minoni Boulevard
Richmond, BC V6X 2A9
(604) 270-9220

Glossary—
Explaining New Words

addiction Physical or emotional dependence on a substance, such as alcohol or other drugs.

Al-Anon A self-help recovery program whose purpose is to help the families and friends of alcoholics deal with problems caused by the alcoholic.

Alateen A self-help recovery program for teenagers whose lives have been affected by their loved ones' drinking.

Alcoholics Anonymous (AA) A fellowship of men and women who share their experiences and problems with alcohol to help themselves and others recover from alcoholism.

alcoholism A disease in which the body becomes physically or psychologically dependent on alcohol.

chemical dependence Strong cravings for a drug that causes people to

60 keep taking the drug even when it is harmful.

cocaine Powerful stimulant of the central nervous system taken from the leaves of the coca plant and made into a powder that is sniffed, smoked, or injected.

Cocaine Anonymous (CA) Community group of cocaine addicts who meet to share their feelings and help one another to stay well and not use cocaine or other drugs.

codependent Someone affected by another person's dependence on alcohol or drugs.

compulsive Happening again and again; uncontrolled need to do something again and again.

denial Unwillingness to admit the truth; unwillingness to admit there is a problem with drugs or alcohol.

drug Substance that changes how the mind or body works.

illegal Forbidden by law.

peer A person your own age.

prescription drugs Medicines that must be ordered by a doctor and prepared by a pharmacist.

speed Street name for amphetamines; also called uppers, pep pills, bennies, dexies, meth, crystal, crank.

For Further Reading

Al-Anon Family Group. *Youth and the Alcoholic Family*. New York: Al-Anon Family Group Headquarters, 1991.

Children of Alcoholics Foundation. *If You Think Your Parent Drinks Too Much . . . .* New York: Children of Alcoholics Foundation, 1992.

Dolmetsch, Paul and Gail Mauricette (eds.). *Teens Talk About Alcohol and Alcoholism*. Garden City, NY: Dolphin/Doubleday, 1987.

Porterfield, Kay Marie. *Coping with an Alcoholic Parent*, rev. ed. New York: Rosen Publishing Group, 1990.

62 | Seixas, Judith. *Living with a Parent Who Takes Drugs*. New York: William and Morrow, 1989.

Shuker, Nancy. *Everything You Need to Know About an Alcoholic Parent*, rev. ed. New York: Rosen Publishing Group, 1993.

Index

About the Author
Rhoda McFarland has taught all grades, kindergarten through twelfth. She is a certified alcoholism and drug abuse counselor, having worked with troubled young people and their parents. She developed and implemented the first educational program in the California area for students making the transition from drug/alcohol treatment programs back into the regular school system. She was a Peace Corps volunteer in Belize, Central America, and then spent four years as a counselor in a high school in the Florida Keys.

Photo Credits
Cover photo by Chuck Peterson; photos on pages 2, 8, 13, 17, 20, 25, 30, 37, 47, 52 by Stuart Rabinowitz; photo on page 40 by Stephanie FitzGerald.